I MET A MAN NAMED DONALD

A Children's Story for Adults, about President Donald Trump

T. H. Logwood

"If you want to act like a child, then I will speak to you as a child"

I WOULD LIKE TO TELL YOU A STORY

Remember the simplicity of reading to your children, conveying an idea in simple words and pictures? Well, maybe as adults, we should do the same.

For the past three or four years, we have watched half of the adults in this country behave like spoiled children. Adults are suppose to have tact and composure when discussing or relating ideas or opinions. Adults are to be role models for our children, in hopes that they will grow up and become like themselves. Adults are supposed to have better manners and speak with some semblance of decency towards one another. These are qualities we hope our own children aspire to.

But what we have seen are Hollywood celebrities, social elites, a biased media, and even many politicians, whining and crying like badly behaved children needing a time-out or a solid spanking. When it comes to anything regarding President Donald Trump, these brats fly off into temper-tantrum mode, basically a state of hysteria, often referred to as "Trump Derangement Syndrome". Anything this adult man does, comes with disdainful hateful potty-mouth outbursts and opposition from these people, making the rest of us scratch our heads with disbelief. What in the world is going on here?

Ever since Donald J. Trump rode the escalator down to announce his candidacy for president of the United States in 2015, these "spoiled children" have done and said everything they could to stand in his way. He was dully elected the 45th President of the United States, by the Will of the People, according to our laws and Constitutional foundation. But for those, that reality has never been accepted. Look, grow up and get over yourselves, it happened. Now lets get on with business and life, and "Make America Great Again" (to quote then candidate Trump). It is time to act like the adults we are suppose to be.

And for over three years, these "brats", and most of the democrats in congress have obstructed every action President Trump has taken to fulfill the promises he made to the people. The democrats have done nothing but lie, cheat, and obstructed, the President in his duty to make our country (and the people) better. The Dems have thrown every deceitful trick in the book to halt this president's agenda, spending millions and millions of tax-payer dollars, yet have done nothing at all to serve their own constituents, nor the good of the country. It is shameful beyond shame, and yet these clowns are elected to public office to rule over us?

Have they succeeded? I think not, listen to this story. Since many adults want to behave like children, then perhaps a story can be read to them, as children.

I MET A MAN
NAMED DONALD

I was traveling across America, and I met a man named Donald. He was dressed in a fine dark blue suit, with shiny black shoes, and bright red tie. His complexion was fair, his smile bright, but he had a funny golden wave of hair on his head.

He looked important, maybe a movie-star or a host from a TV show, yet he spoke like my cousin, with a slight Manhattan accent. He couldn't be a politician, he sure didn't talk like one, or make promises like them.

Still there was something unique and different to him that caught my interest. It wasn't his fancy clothes, or his big expensive car, nor his ravishingly gorgeous wife by his side, but there was something else I liked.

I asked him, "The people are discouraged, and we are viewed

poorly by the rest of the world. Can you change that?"

He said, "Yes. I will restore the Pride and Honor of America."

[Since Trump became President, he supported our Veterans, stood up firmly to world leaders, brought about jobs and a strong economy for a man can work for his own needs. He has supported and uplifted the American people, their goodness and virtues, uniting the people as best he could.]

Restored

I was traveling across America, and I met a man named Donald.

I asked him, "The politicians we elect spend our money and do nothing but get fat and rich. Can you fix that?"

He said, "Yes. I will find out Who they are, and I will "Drain the Swamp.""

[Since Trump became President, he brought about the truth of the crimes and corruption of the former administration, the "soft coup" to overthrow the 2016 election, exposed the cesspool of corruption within the State Department, intelligence community, and other agencies.]

Restored
Exposed

I was traveling across America, and I met a man named Donald.

I asked him, "We are weary of sending our young men to fight needless wars, and worry about terrorists. Can you help us?"

He said, "Yes. I will talk with foreign leaders, and squash the terrorist threats."

[Since Trump became President, he brought home many of our troops, unleashed the military might to crush ISIS and other radical groups. Conflict will be handled more with the hi-tech weaponry than the foot soldier. He met with many world leaders and made our intentions clear. Most world leaders now admire and respect our country as a strong force for good and decent goals.]

Restored

Exposed

Ended

I was traveling across America, and I met a man named Donald.

I asked him, "There are not enough jobs, and many people are struggling to get by. Can you help?"

He said, "Yes. I will loosen the reigns of government, end needless regulations, and cut taxes."

[Since Trump became President, hundreds of needless and burdensome regulations have been eliminated, the largest tax cut in American history was enacted, and manufacturing jobs are coming back to our country. Record high stock market values, indicating the increased prosperity of the economy. Record low unemployment, higher wages, lower taxes, are results of turning his turning around the economy.]

ReStored
EXposed

ENded
LooSeNed

I was traveling across America, and I met a man named Donald.

I asked him, "Why are the laws not enforced? People from other countries are pouring across our border, yet former leaders wouldn't stop it".

He said, "Yes. I will build a wall, and direct the leaders to follow the rules. I will appoint good judges and officials to strengthen the laws."

[Since Trump became President, he has built hundreds of miles of border wall, greatly stopped most of the illegals crossing the border. Directed law enforcement to catch and deport criminals, provided funding to protect our borders. He has appointed about 190 federal court judges, that will also enforce the due process of law.]

ReStored
EXpoSed

ENded
LooSeNed
ENForced

I was traveling across America, and I met a man named Donald.

I asked him, "If the Constitution is our founding document, why are our Rights and Freedoms being restricted?"

He said, "Yes. I will can change that. I will appoint constitutional originalist justices to the Supreme Court."

[Since Trump became President, he has had two Supreme Court Justices confirmed. They are Judges that will abide and uphold the Constitutional foundation and intent of the Founding Fathers, not cower to the emotional fads of the day. If our fundamental core Rights are upheld by the highest court in the land, it trickles down to every part of our lives.]

ReStored
ExpoSed

ENded
LooSeNed
ENForced
CoNFirMed

I was traveling across America, and I met a man named Donald.

I asked him, "On the news and in the movies, I hear how awful it is to be an American. The people are divided. Can you change that?"

He said, "Yes. I have been working on that, but there is still much work to be done. I will need your vote in November to "Keep America Great"."

[Since Trump became President, he has done a great volume of work to restore the health and vitality of the nation, despite the democrats and opposition groups. Many more people have a renewed hope in their daily lives, and overall much better than we have been for many years.]

Restored
Exposed

Ended
Loosened
Enforced
Confirmed
Turned Around

And just as I was about to leave, He asked me, "Who are you?"

I said, "I was the voice of the forgotten American. Thank you hearing me."

And at last, I figured out what I liked... he was Honest. After all of the campaigning, fighting for the American people, and suffering through the endless borage of criticism, he remains an Honest Politician. He is "a breath of fresh air", and worthy of my vote.

R E ELECT Donald

THE ACCOMPLISHMENTS OF PRESIDENT TRUMP

As of this publication, these are many of the actions and accomplishments completed and undertaken by President Trump. Although not a 100% listing of them, it is significantly more than the "fake and biased media" will ever give him credit for. He has worked for the American people, kept his campaign promises (unlike many politicians), and has in reality set the machinery of action to turn this nation around (in a good and positive direction). President Donald Trump has "Made this country Great again."

For a non-politician, businessman, to get elected to the most powerful office in the world, make promises to the people, and do them, is truly amazing in this era. To you President Trump, we say, "Kudos" and Thanks!

In his first three years in office, President Trump has (Summarized):

*** About 4 million jobs created since his election.**

*** More Americans employed than ever recorded.**

*** More than 400,000 manufacturing jobs since his election.**

* Fastest manufacturing jobs growth rate in over 30 years.

* Economic growth averaging about 4% (last quarter had 4.2%).

* New unemployment claims dropped to a 49-year low.

* Median household income reached the highest level ever recorded.

* African-American unemployment rate is at the lowest level ever recorded.

* Hispanic-American unemployment is at the lowest level ever recorded.

* Asian-American unemployment also is at the lowest level ever recorded.

* Women's unemployment rate is at the lowest level in 65 years.

* Youth unemployment has also dropped to the lowest level in almost 50 years.

* And for Americans without a high school diploma, the lowest unemployment level ever recorded.

* Veterans also have reached the lowest unemployment level in nearly 20 years.

* Nearly 4 million Americans have been lifted off food stamps since his election.

* U.S. manufacturers are optimistic about the future, with 95% positive rating, the highest ever.

* Retail sales are up another 6% over last year.

* Trump signed into law, the largest package of tax cuts and reforms in history. After tax cuts, over $300 billion poured back in to the U.S. in the first quarter alone.

* Small businesses have the lowest top marginal tax rate in more than 80 years.

* Brought America back to energy independence.

* Opened ANWR and approved Keystone XL and Dakota Access Pipelines.

* Record number of federal regulations eliminated.

* Enacted regulatory relief for community banks and credit unions.

* The Affordable Care Act (Obamacare) individual mandate penalty was eliminated.

* His Administration is providing more affordable healthcare options for Americans through association health plans and short-term duration plans.

* Got the FDA to approve more affordable generic drugs than ever before in history.

* He reformed the Medicare program to stop hospitals from overcharging low-income seniors on their prescriptions.

* Signed Right-To-Try legislation.

* Secured $6 billion in new funding to fight the opioid

epidemic.

* Signed into law, the VA Choice Act and VA Accountability Act, expanded VA tele-health services, walk-in-clinics, and same-day urgent primary and mental health care.

* Increased our coal exports by 60%, and U.S. oil production has reached an all-time high.

* United States is a net exporter for natural gas, the first time since 1957.

* Withdrew the United States from the wasteful job-killing Paris Climate Accord.

* Cancelled the illegal, anti-coal, so-called Clean Power Plan.

* He secured a record $700 billion in military funding last year, and $716 billion next year.

* NATO allies are spending $69 billion more on defense since 2016.

* Made the Space Force, the 6th branch of the Armed Forces.

* Confirmed more than 190 federal and circuit court judges.

* Confirmed Supreme Court Justices Neil Gorsuch and Judge Brett Kavanaugh.

* Withdrew from the unenforceable Iran Deal.

* Moved the U.S. Embassy to Jerusalem (Israel's capital).

* Increased American protection from terrorists with the Travel Ban (upheld by Supreme Court).

* Issued an Executive Order to keep open Guantanamo Bay.

* Replaced NAFTA with the USMCA, a historic U.S.-Mexico Trade Deal.

* Reached a breakthrough deal with the European Union to increase U.S. exports.

* Imposed tariffs on foreign steel and aluminum to protect our national security.

* Imposed tariffs on China in response to China's forced technology transfer, intellectual property theft, and their chronically abusive trade practices.

* Made the first-round of a new China Trade deal, and working on a trade deal with Great Britain.

* Net exports have increased about $59 billion this year.

* Improved vetting and screening for refugees, and switched focus to overseas resettlement.

* Has secured funding for the southern border wall, with hundreds of miles completed. He has increased ICE and border security, and has deported many "bad hombres" (to quote the president).

(This is a summarized list obtained from the White House website. Any internet search can offer a more in-depth list of actual accomplishments.)

A COUPLE FINAL THOUGHTS

Elections have consequences. If politicians are elected, who have the directive to fulfill the desires of the people, they will enact laws to uphold or eliminate the rights and privileges we hold. If we elect leaders that adhere to our Founding Fathers that formulated our Constitution, great, that makes for a happy and productive nation. However, if we elect those who have a different agenda or ideology, we can lose our Rights and Freedoms as guaranteed under the Constitution. Our vote is our voice. It is the most simple and basic duty every citizen has in this country.

Our system of government was designed and set up to assure the people would have the liberty to become all they can aspire to become. The freedom of free and open speech, and religious liberties, backed up by the ability to bear arms, has been the cornerstone of this country, rooted in the process of free and open elections. Every vote counts, and every citizen has a duty to make this country better, according to their own conscience.

The trend in our elections and the types of people elected to office is actually very scary. Donald Trump has been a welcomed respite to the dark downward spiral this country was headed. Too many candidates, social elitists, organizations, and segments of the population are pushing for a government-led, governmental-controlled society. Free health care, free schooling, gun restrictions, abortion on demand, and so on, all have great costs. Nothing is free. The costs come from high taxation of the working man, but also through the limitations imposed on our liberties to make choices and decisions for ourselves. Power of the people given over to the control of a few, spells disaster for a nation.

Does anyone remember the rise of Nazi Germany, Stalinist Russia, or the rise of Maoist China? Are such things no longer taught in our public schools? With the promises of good intentions for the people, power concentrated in the hands of the few, which brought about a reign of bloodshed and destruction of the nations. Let not history repeat itself.

For example, our Constitution guarantees the rights to bear arms, the freedom to worship God as we like, the ability speak openly in opposition of the government or laws that are enacted, our rights to join together in public, and more. But all of our Rights and Freedoms are gravely at risk of being taken away. It is through the people we vote into office. Those leaders then push for laws that restricts personal choices and liberties, in favor of government controlled choice. This is true and becoming more so, in every facet of our lives. Just look at all of the laws and regulations we live with every day. Not that you particularly notice them, but there are thousands if not tens of thousands or regulations that restricts our freedoms. This has been the trend for the past fifty or so years. If our Founders could only see the degradation of their intent, they would call for a new revolution. As we lose our freedom of speech (again as an example), we become slaves to the government.

Power and control unchecked, will destroy a nation. What happens in every nation, documented throughout history, is that "power corrupts". Machiavelli, back in the 1500's said in his book, "the Prince", that power corrupts, and absolute power corrupts absolutely". As power becomes concentrated in the hands of a few, they abuse it. Then the rulers oppress the people (through laws, regulation, and brutality). Finally, due to opposition, the rulers mass murder their own citizens to maintain their power. Gratefully, our Founders divided the centers of powers, each as a check upon the other. At least it is suppose to be that way.

As our society writhes with turmoil over the legalities of guns and life, the next election cycle approaches. Many groups are seeking to undermine our rights and liberties, including over-turning parts of the Constitution itself. Although the Constitution is "set in stone", so to speak, having liberal or modern-thinking Supreme Court justices on the bench can interpret the laws contrary to originalist precedence. It is critical for the survival of the nation as a whole; to learn about the candidates and what they value, and stand with those who think the same as yourself. This is no time for any American to sit idle, there is just too much at stake.

There is a little story that is important to keep in mind.

"A bunch of sheep were happily grazing in the field, enjoying the comforts of their lives. A wolf came out of the woods and killed one of the sheep. In a panic, they formed a consensus on what to do. They decided the best way to keep themselves safe was to remove all of their teeth. Later, the wolf came back and killed them all."

Set that clearly in your mind. Laws only work if they are enforced, and, if everyone follows them. Those who are unlawful, do not follow the laws. So be wary of whom you elect to office.

ABOUT THE AUTHOR

I grew up in a middle class family, had a father that worked, a mother that stayed home and raised children, the typical traditional American home. We had a small house, one car, (no) white picket fence, we had pets, guns, regular schooling, church-goers, watched news and various TV shows, hunted and shot targets, and had all of the cliche normal things in life typified during the 1950s and 60s. Life was normal and decent, reasonably peaceful, and safe.

My father was a veteran, worked a blue collar job, and was a straight-line democrat, just like his father before him. The Kennedy era thinking of party politics was pretty much his thinking as well. And for many decades, that seemed to work well in America. I too learned and adopted similar ideas of how life and government should work and coexist.

But that has changed radically over the past couple decades, as the democrat party is no longer the party of the average working man. One would best describe the party as what we used to call the Communist-Socialist party during that earlier era. Now the party is all about hate speech, bigotry, division, dirty-politics, rampant dishonesty and deception by party leaders and candidates, and everything revolving around government control. This is no longer the democrat party America once loved.

The candidates and false narratives they promoted were enough to make me switch to the Republican Party. Over the last many election cycles while the democrats drove further left, I pushed my family and friends to switch parties and vote further right.

Not that the republicans are perfect by any means, but they do hold to more of the values and principles I do. The biggest area where they align with my own thinking are the ideas of limited government, the sanctity of life, and support for the Constitution. Upholding our rights and freedoms are more their forte, so this is where we will stay.

My hope is to share these thoughts with you, so that you can glean some insight of the struggle we face over our dying liberties. Thank you reading this.

Also consider these other books written about our Rights and Freedoms. These also are found on Amazon Kindle under the Politics section. Look for:

"Don't Tread on Me"
By T. H. Logwood
ASIN: B07X5DRRYB

*****

"The Democrat Blue Wave is the Zombie Apocalypse"
by T. H. Logwood
ASIN: B07MYBFKT1

*****

"Repent America, In the Name of Jesus!"
By T. H. Logwood
ASIN: B07NBXYLLB

*****

"The End of American Liberty"
By T. H. Logwood
ASIN: B07HPYZWTF

*****

"The Democrat Blue Wave is the Texas 2nd Alamo"

By T. H. Logwood
ASIN: B07N7N2WG6

* * * * *

"The End of American Freedom"
By T. H. Logwood
ASIN: B07MSJ4QD7

* * * * *

"The U.S.S. La Porte (APA 151), The Pearl of the Pacific"
By T. H. Logwood
ASIN: B07L6JXRB9

* * * * *

"A Walk in the Sub-Alpine Meadows: A Look at the Tuoloume Meadows Ecosystem"
By T. H. Logwood
ASIN: B07HM928TH

* * * * *

"Collecting Old Stock Certificates: A Look at the Past"
By T. H. Logwood
ASIN: B07HNX1FGK

www.ingramcontent.com/pod-product-compliance
Lightning Source LLC
Chambersburg PA
CBHW051143250726

48655CB00007B/3212